ESSENTIAL COMPUTERS

WORD PROCESSING

LETTERS & MAILING

JOSHUA MOSTAFA

DK

LONDON, NEW YORK, MUNICH,
MELBOURNE, DELHI

SENIOR EDITOR Jacky Jackson
SENIOR ART EDITOR Sarah Cowley
DTP DESIGNER Julian Dams and Rajen Shah
PRODUCTION CONTROLLER Melanie Dowland

MANAGING EDITOR Adèle Hayward
MANAGING ART EDITOR Karen Self
CATEGORY PUBLISHER Stephanie Jackson

Produced for Dorling Kindersley Limited by
Design Revolution Limited, Queens Park Villa,
30 West Drive, Brighton, East Sussex BN2 0QW
EDITORIAL DIRECTOR Ian Whitelaw
SENIOR DESIGNER Andrew Easton
PROJECT EDITOR John Watson
DESIGNER Paul Bowler

First published in Great Britain in 2000 by
Dorling Kindersley Limited,
80 Strand, London WC2R 0RL

Revised edition 2002
A Penguin publication

2 4 6 8 10 9 7 5 3 1

A CIP catalogue record for this book is available from the British Library.

ISBN 0-7513-4631-4

Colour reproduced by Colourscan, Singapore
Printed and bound in Italy by Graphicom

For our complete catalogue visit
www.dk.com

CONTENTS

MICROSOFT WORD

Microsoft Word has been around for well over a decade and, with each new release, adds to its reputation as the world's leading word-processing program.

WHAT CAN WORD DO?

The features contained in Word make it one of the most flexible word-processing programs available. Word can be used to write anything from shopping lists to large publications that contain, in addition to the main text, illustrations and graphics, charts, tables and graphs, captions, headers and footers, cross references, footnotes, indexes, and glossaries – all of which are easily managed by Word. Word can check spelling and grammar, check text readability, search and replace text, import data, sort data, perform calculations, and provide templates for many types of documents from memos to web pages. The comprehensive and versatile design, formatting, and layout options in Word make it ideal for desktop publishing on almost any scale. In short, there's very little that Word cannot do.

WHAT IS A WORD DOCUMENT?

In its simplest form, a Word document is a sequence of characters that exists in a computer's memory. Using Word, a document can be edited, added to, and given a variety of layouts. Once the document has been created, there are a large number of actions that can be carried out, such as saving, printing, or sending the document as an email.

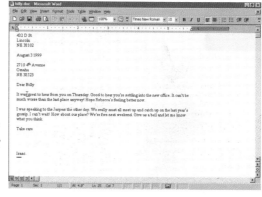

LAUNCHING WORD

Word launches just like any other program running in Windows. With the Windows desktop onscreen, you can launch Word as the only program running, or you can run Word alongside other software to exchange data with other applications.

1 LAUNCHING BY THE START MENU

● Place the mouse cursor over the **Start** button on the Taskbar and click with the left mouse button.

● Move the cursor up the pop-up menu until **Programs** is highlighted. A submenu of programs appears to the right.

● Move the cursor down the menu to **Microsoft Word** and left-click again. (If **Microsoft Word** is missing from the **Programs** menu, it may be under **Microsoft Office**.)

● The **Microsoft Word** window opens △.

2 LAUNCHING BY A SHORTCUT

● You may already have a Word icon onscreen, which is a shortcut to launching Word. If so, double-click on the icon.

● The Microsoft Word window opens △.

THE WORD WINDOW

At first, Word's document window may look like a space shuttle computer display. However, you'll soon discover that similar commands and actions are neatly grouped together. This "like-with-like" layout helps you quickly understand where you should be looking on the window for what you want. Click and play while you read this.

THE WORD WINDOW

1 Title bar
2 Menu bar
Contains the main menus.
3 Standard toolbar
Buttons for frequent actions.
4 Formatting toolbar
Main layout options.
5 Tab selector
Clicking selects type of tab.
6 Left-indent buttons
Used to set left indents.
7 Ruler
Displays margins and tabs.
8 Right-indent button
Used to set right indent.
9 Insertion point
Shows where typing appears.
10 Text area
Area for document text.
11 Split box
Creates two text panes.
12 Scroll-up arrow
Moves up the document.
13 Scroll-bar box
Moves text up or down.
14 Vertical scroll bar
Used to move through text.

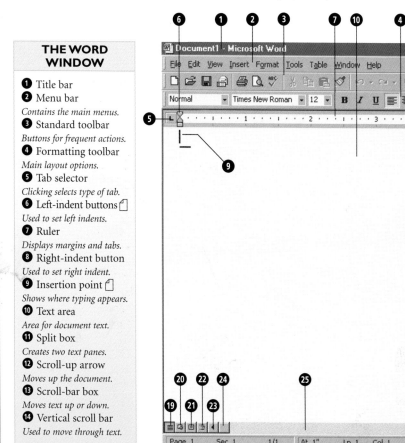

| 12 | **Insertion point** |
| 30 | **Indenting the Address** |

TOOLBAR LAYOUT

If Word doesn't show the Formatting toolbar below the Standard toolbar, first place the cursor over the Formatting toolbar "handle." When the four-headed arrow appears, (right) hold down the mouse button and "drag" the toolbar into position.

THE WORD WINDOW

15 Scroll-down arrow
Moves down the document.

16 Page-up button
Shows previous page of text.

17 Select browse object
Opens browse options menu.

18 Page-down button
Displays next page of text.

19 Normal view
Default document view.

20 Web layout view
Web-browser page view.

21 Page layout view
Printed-page view of text.

22 Outline view
Shows document's structure.

23 Left-scroll arrow
Shows the text to the left.

24 Scroll-bar box
Moves text horizontally.

25 Horizontal scroll bar
To view wide documents.

26 Right-scroll arrow
Shows the text to the right.

27 Language
Spelling, thesaurus, and proofing settings.

THE WORD TOOLBARS

Word provides a range of toolbars where numerous commands and actions are available. The principal toolbars are the Standard toolbar and the Formatting toolbar, which contain the most frequently used features of Word. There are also more than 20 other toolbars available for display. Click on **Tools** in the Menu bar, move the cursor down to **Customize**, and click the mouse button. The **Customize** dialog box opens. Click the Toolbars tab to view the variety of toolbars available.

THE STANDARD TOOLBAR

- ❶ New document
- ❷ Open folder or file
- ❸ Save
- ❹ Email
- ❺ Print
- ❻ Print preview
- ❼ Spelling and grammar
- ❽ Cut text
- ❾ Copy text
- ❿ Paste text
- ⓫ Format painter
- ⓬ Undo action(s)
- ⓭ Redo action(s)
- ⓮ Insert hyperlink
- ⓯ Tables and borders
- ⓰ Insert table
- ⓱ Insert Excel worksheet
- ⓲ Columns
- ⓳ Drawing toolbar
- ⓴ Document map
- ㉑ Show/hide formatting marks
- ㉒ Zoom view of text
- ㉓ Microsoft Word help

CUSTOMIZING A TOOLBAR

To add a **Close** button to a toolbar, click on the **Commands** tab of the **Customize** box (see left). Place the cursor over the **Close** icon, hold down the mouse button, drag the icon to the toolbar, and release the mouse button.

ScreenTips
It isn't necessary to memorize all these buttons. Roll the cursor over a button, wait for a second, and a ScreenTip appears telling you the function of the button.

THE FORMATTING TOOLBAR

- **24** Style selector
- **25** Font selector
- **26** Font size selector
- **27** Bold
- **28** Italic
- **29** Underline
- **30** Left-aligned text
- **31** Centered text
- **32** Right-aligned text
- **33** Justified text
- **34** Numbered list
- **35** Bulleted list
- **36** Decrease indent
- **37** Increase indent
- **38** Outside border
- **39** Highlight color
- **40** Font color
- **41** Minimize Word
- **42** Restore Word
- **43** Close Word
- **44** Close document

35 | Quick ways to align text

36 | Font and Font Size

36 | Quick ways to format fonts

YOUR FIRST LETTER

Microsoft Word makes the process of writing a letter and printing it out easier than ever. This chapter takes you through the few simple steps involved in creating your first letter.

TYPING THE LETTER

The first image on your screen when you start Microsoft Word is a blank area with a blinking cursor, surrounded by buttons and symbols that may mean nothing to you. Don't worry about them for now. To begin with, the only thing you need to concentrate on is to start writing your letter on that blank screen.

1 BEGINNING TYPING

● Type the first line of your address. As you type, the insertion point moves with your text. Don't worry about mistakes – they are easily corrected ⌐.

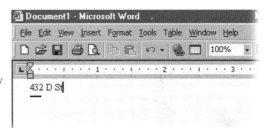

2 STARTING A NEW LINE

● Press the Enter ↵ button.
● The insertion point has now moved to the beginning of a new line.

Insertion point ●

INSERTION POINT

This is a blinking upright line that precedes your text as you type. If you are ever unsure about where your typing will appear on the page, check where the insertion point is.

⌐ **Correcting Errors as You Type** 14

3 COMPLETING THE ADDRESS

● Finish typing your address, pressing [Enter ←] at the end of each line.
● At the end of the last address line, press [Enter ←] twice to leave a line space.

432 D St
Lincoln
NE 38102

4 STARTING THE LETTER

● Now type the date, leave another line space, then type the recipient's address.
● Leave two lines (by pressing [Enter ←] three times) and type your greeting.

432 D St
Lincoln
NE 38102

August 3 1999

2710 4ᵗʰ Avenue
Omaha
NE 38523

Dear Billy

5 CREATING PARAGRAPHS

● Leave another line and start your first paragraph. When typing paragraphs in Word, just keep typing until the end of the paragraph, and only then press [Enter ←]. At the end of each line, Word "wraps" your text round to start a new line.
● To start a new paragraph, press [Enter ←] to end the first paragraph, and press [Enter ←] again to leave a line space. You are ready to start the new paragraph.

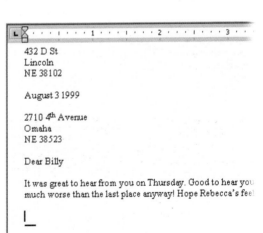

432 D St
Lincoln
NE 38102

August 3 1999

2710 4ᵗʰ Avenue
Omaha
NE 38523

Dear Billy

It was great to hear from you on Thursday. Good to hear you
much worse than the last place anyway! Hope Rebecca's fee

6 FINISHING THE LETTER

● If your letter is longer than can fit on the screen, Word moves the text up as you type. If you need to go back to it, simply hold down the ⬆ arrow key. The insertion point moves up the text to the top of your letter.

● Type a farewell after the last paragraph. Press Enter⏎ a few times to leave room for your signature. Then type your name.

● You have now typed your first letter using Word.

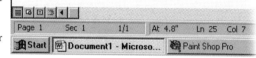

much worse than the last place anyway! Hope Rebecca's fee

I was speaking to the Jaspers the other day. We really must a gossip. How about our place? We're free next weekend. Giv think.

Take care

Isaac

Page 1   Sec 1   1/1   At 4.8"   Ln 25   Col 7

Start   Document1 - Microso...   Paint Shop Pro

CORRECTING ERRORS AS YOU TYPE

1 REMOVING THE ERROR

● You have misspelled a word as you are typing.

● To remove the misspelled word, first press the Backspace (← Bksp) key. This removes text one letter at a time to the left of the insertion point.

● Keep tapping ← Bksp until the word is gone.

Dear Billy

It was great to hear from you on Thursday. Good to hear you much worse than the last place anyway! Hope Rebecca's feel

I was speaking to the Jaspers the other day. We really must a gossip. How aubot

Dear Billy

It was great to hear from you on Thursday. Good to hear you much worse than the last place anyway! Hope Rebecca's feel

I was speaking to the Jaspers the other day. We really must a gossip. How

2 REPLACING THE ERROR

● Now type the word again. Remember to leave a space before it – ⌐← Bksp⌐ also removes spaces and line spaces if they are immediately to the left of the insertion point.

● You have corrected the error and you can carry on typing your letter.

Dear Billy

It was great to hear from you on Thursday. Good to hear you much worse than the last place anyway! Hope Rebecca's fee

I was speaking to the Jaspers the other day. We really must gossip. How about|

FORMATTING MARKS

Word uses invisible markers (called formatting marks) within your text to mark the spaces between words, and where you have decided to leave line spaces. Formatting marks do not appear on paper when you print out. Initially you don't see them on your screen,

which makes the text on the screen appear exactly how it will print out. However, you may want to see the formatting marks so that you can see double spaces and control where you want the line spaces to be placed. To see the formatting marks, click on the small, down-arrow button in the middle of your toolbar. A

menu drops down. Click on the button with the paragraph mark. You are now able to see the formatting marks. Click the button again when you want to turn off the formatting marks. You won't need to drop down the menu again – after the first use, Word adds the button to your toolbar.

CORRECTING ERRORS FROM EARLIER IN THE TEXT

It is inevitable that errors are made as you type, such as misspellings and duplicate words. If you notice an error higher up in your letter than where you are currently typing, you can move the insertion point back to the error and easily correct it.

1 MOVING TO THE ERROR

● The misspelled word is higher in the text than the insertion point. You may be familiar with using the mouse to relocate the insertion point, but you may be less familiar with using the arrow keys.

● Move the insertion point up to the line containing the error by using the ↑ arrow key.

● Use the ← and → arrow keys until you've placed the insertion point at the end of the misspelled word.

It was great to hear from you on Thursday. Good to hear you much worse than the last place anyway! Hope Rebecca's fee

I was spaeking to the Jaspers the other day. We really must gossip. How about our place? We're free next weekend. Giv think

It was great to hear from you on Thursday. Good to hear you much worse than the last place anyway! Hope Rebecca's fee

I was spaeking to the Jaspers the other day. We really must gossip. How about our place? We're free next weekend. Giv think.

2 CORRECTING THE ERROR

● Remove the misspelled word and type it in with the correct spelling.

● You have now corrected the error. Use the ↓ arrow key to return the insertion point to where you left off. You can now continue with your typing.

It was great to hear from you on Thursday. Good to hear you much worse than the last place anyway! Hope Rebecca's fee

I was speaking to the Jaspers the other day. We really must gossip. How about our place? We're free next weekend. Giv think.

ADDING WORDS IN THE MIDDLE OF THE TEXT

Word makes it easy for you to change your text at any time while writing your letter. If you decide to add something further, or suddenly realize that an important point has been left out, you can type it in by first using the insertion point.

1 POSITIONING THE INSERTION POINT

● Move the insertion point to the place in the text where you want to add words. Use the arrow keys on your keyboard again for further practice. Remember, you can only move to where text has already been typed.

Insertion point ●

Omaha
NE 38523

Dear Billy

It was great to hear from you on Thursday. Good to hear you much worse than the last place anyway! Hope Rebecca's fee

I was speaking to the Jaspers the other day. We really must gossip. How about our place? We're free next weekend. Giv think.

Take care

Isaac.

2 ADDING THE WORDS

● Start typing the new text. If the insertion point is in the middle of a paragraph, you'll notice that Word automatically moves text along to accommodate what you are adding.
● Use the arrow keys to return to the place where you left off typing.

Omaha
NE 38523

Dear Billy

It was great to hear from you on Thursday. Good to hear you much worse than the last place anyway! Hope Rebecca's fee

I was speaking to the Jaspers the other day. We really must gossip. I can't wait! How about our place? We're free next w what you think.

Take care

MANIPULATING PARAGRAPHS

Paragraphs organize your text, help with the sense of your document, and make your document more readable. With Word it's easy to create a new paragraph when another is needed, and to combine them when two paragraphs aren't required.

1 SPLITTING A PARAGRAPH

● To split a paragraph into two, move the insertion point to the start of the sentence that will begin the new second paragraph. Then press [Enter ←] twice. You now have two paragraphs.

I was speaking to the Jaspers the other day. We really must a gossip. I can't wait! How about our place? We're free next v what you think.

Take care

I was speaking to the Jaspers the other day. We really must a gossip. I can't wait!

How about our place? We're free next weekend. Give us a b

Take care

2 COMBINING PARAGRAPHS

● If you want to join two paragraphs together to make one, place the insertion point at the beginning of the second paragraph. Then press [← Bksp] twice to remove the line spaces. Your two paragraphs now form one larger paragraph.

It was great to hear from you on Thursday. Good to hear you're settling into the new office. It c much worse than the last place anyway! Hope Rebecca's feeling better now.

I was speaking to the Jaspers the other day. We really must all meet up and catch up on the last gossip. I can't wait! How about our place? We're free next weekend. Give us a bell and let me l what you think.

Take care

3 PARAGRAPH MARKS

● Pressing the [Enter ←] key ends a paragraph and inserts a paragraph mark. You can see these marks by turning on the formatting marks 🗋. Deleting the line space between paragraphs is just a matter of deleting the paragraph mark just like any other character.

It was great to hear from you on Thursday. Good to hear you're settling into the new office. It c
much worse than the last place anyway! Hope Rebecca's feeling better now. I was speaking to
Jaspers the other day. We really must all meet up and catch up on the last year's gossip. I can't
wait! How about our place? We're free next weekend. Give us a bell and let me know what you

Take care

USING WORD TO START A NEW PAGE

If you want to begin a new page, before the text has reached the end of the current page, you can use Word to split the page into two.

Move the insertion point to the position in your letter where you want the new page to start. Hold down the [Ctrl] key and press [Enter ←]. Word inserts a "manual" page break. You can delete this page break by placing the insertion point at the top left of the second page and pressing [← Bksp].

Dear Billy

It was great to hear from you on Thursday. Good to hear you're settling into the new office. I
much worse than the last place anyway! Hope Rebecca's feeling better now.

I was speaking to the Jaspers the other day. We really must all meet up and catch up on the l
gossip. I can't wait! How about our place? We're free next weekend. Give us a bell and let me
what you think.

Dear Billy

It was great to hear from you on Thursday. Good to hear you're settling into the new office. I
much worse than the last place anyway! Hope Rebecca's feeling better now.
·····Page Break·····

I was speaking to the Jaspers the other day. We really must all meet up and catch up on the l
gossip. I can't wait! How about our place? We're free next weekend. Give us a bell and let me
what you think.

---

15 **Formatting marks**

SAVING YOUR LETTER

Now that your letter is finished and correct, you should save it as a file on your computer's hard disk so that if you need to find it later, or make changes after you have printed it out, you will be able to bring it back up on the screen.

1 SAVING THE FILE

● Move your mouse pointer over the word **File** in the Menu bar at the top of the screen. Click on **File** and the File menu drops down. Move the mouse pointer down and click on **Save**.

● The **Save As** dialog box pops up in the middle of your screen. In this box you are able to give your letter a file name and decide where you want to save it on the hard disk.

2 NAMING AND SAVING

● Choose a file name that identifies the letter for you and type it into the **File name** box.

● Select a folder in the **Save in** box and click on the **Save** button. The dialog box closes and your letter is saved to disk.

PRINTING YOUR LETTER

1 FILE PRINT

● Click on the **File** menu. The **File** menu drops down.
● This time choose **Print** from the File menu by clicking once on **Print**.

2 PRINT YOUR LETTER

● The **Print** dialog box pops up. Don't worry about any of the features here at this stage. Just make sure that the printer is plugged into the computer and is switched on.
● Click on the **OK** button at the bottom of the dialog box and your letter begins to print.

Well done…
You have now typed, corrected, saved, and printed your first letter using Word. These simple steps have shown you the basic process that you use to create a letter with Microsoft Word. Now we go into more detail and explore each step of the process in detail.

WORKING WITH TEXT

This section deals with methods of working with text: moving around text, shifting text from one place to another, deleting text, and copying text.

MOVING AROUND YOUR TEXT

There are many different ways to move around and see different parts of your letter. Here are some techniques to move through your letter that make use of either the mouse or the different actions that are available through the keyboard.

1 GET TO THE START OF THE LETTER

● The insertion point is midway through or at the end of the letter.
● Hold down the [Ctrl] key and press the [Home] key on your keyboard.
● The screen now shows the top of the letter. The insertion point is at the very beginning of the text.

The insertion point moves to the start of the letter

Dear Billy

It was great to hear from you on Thursday. Good to hear yo
much worse than the last place anyway! Hope Rebecca's fee

I was speaking to the Jaspers the other day. We really must a
gossip. I can't wait! How about our place? We're free next w
what you think.

Take care

432 D St
Lincoln
NE 38102

August 3 1999

2710 4th Avenue
Omaha
NE 38523

Dear Billy

2 GET TO THE END OF THE TEXT

● Hold down the `Ctrl` key and press the `End` key on your keyboard.
● The screen now shows the foot of the letter. The insertion point is at the very end of the text.

I was speaking to the Jaspers the other day. We really must
gossip. I can't wait! How about our place? We're free next
what you think.

Take care

Isaac

3 SCROLLING THROUGH TEXT

● If you can't see the part of the letter you want, position the mouse cursor over the sliding box in the scroll bar.

Hold down the left mouse button and move the box up and down the bar to scroll through the text.
● Alternatively, use the buttons at the top and

bottom of the scroll bar. Click on them to scroll the text up and down.
● Stop when the section of the text appears that you want to work on.

● *Scroll bar button*

● *Scroll bar sliding box*

new office. It can't be

h up on the last year's
bell and let me know

MOVING AROUND WITHOUT THE MOUSE

If you want to move quickly around your letter without using the mouse, you can use the `PgUp` and `PgDn` keys on your keyboard to move up or down your letter one screen at a time. This method moves the insertion point directly. You can use the arrow keys to place the insertion point in the exact position in the text where you need to make your changes.

4 CLICKING ON TEXT

● Move the mouse pointer to the exact point in the text where you want the insertion point to go.
● Left-click once. The insertion point appears.

Dear Billy

It was great to hear from you on Thursday. Good to hear you
much worse than the last place anyway! Hope Rebecca's fee

I was speaking to the Jaspers the other day. We really must a
gossip. I can't wait! How about our place? We're free next w
what you think.

Take care

SELECTING TEXT

Before Word can carry out any changes that you want to make, you first need to tell Word what parts of the text you want it to work on. This is done by selecting text, which is one of the most frequently used operations when using Word.

1 USING THE KEYBOARD

● Move the insertion point to the start of the text you want to select.
● Hold down the ⇧ Shift key and press the → arrow key. This has the effect of creating a block of selected text one letter at a time.

It was great to hear from you on Thursday. Good to hear you
much worse than the last place anyway! Hope Rebecca's fee

I was speaking to the Jaspers the other day. We really must a
gossip. I can't wait! How about our place? We're free next w
what you think.

Take care

It was great to hear from you on Thursday. Good to hear you
much worse than the last place anyway! Hope Rebecca's fee

I was speaking to the Jaspers the other day. We really must a
gossip. I can't wait! How about our place? We're free next w
what you think.

Take care

● If the block you want to select extends over more than one line, keep the ⟨⟨ Shift⟩ key held down, and press the ⟨ ↓ ⟩ key to select whole lines at a time. Then use the ⟨ ← ⟩ and ⟨ → ⟩ keys to choose the end of the block. Don't release the ⟨⟨ Shift⟩ key until you have selected the entire block of text that you want.

Dear Billy

It was great to hear from you on Thursday. Good to hear you much worse than the last place anyway! Hope Rebecca's fee

I was speaking to the Jaspers the other day. We really must gossip. I can't wait! How about our place? We're free next w what you think.

Take care

Vanishing Point

You will notice that when you have selected and highlighted a block of text, there is no longer an insertion point in your Word window. What has happened is that the block of selected text becomes one very large insertion point. It is important to be careful here because if you press any character key on the keyboard while your block is selected, your entire block will vanish and be replaced by whatever you type.

2 USING THE MOUSE

● Move the mouse pointer to the precise point where you want to start your selected block of text.
● Hold down the left mouse button and move the mouse pointer to the position that marks the end of the block that you want.
● Release the mouse button. Your block of text is now selected.
● If you make a mistake, simply click outside the selection and go through the process again.

Dear Billy

It was great to hear from you on Thursday. Good to hear you much worse than the last place anyway! Hope Rebecca's fee

I was speaking to the Jaspers the other day. We really must gossip. I can't wait! How about our place? We're free next v what you think.

Dear Billy

It was great to hear from you on Thursday. Good to hear you much worse than the last place anyway! Hope Rebecca's fee

I was speaking to the Jaspers the other day. We really must gossip. I can't wait! How about our place? We're free next v what you think.

3 SELECTING ALL THE TEXT

● Click on **Edit** on the menu bar. The **Edit** menu drops down.

● Now click on **Select All** in the **Edit** menu.

● The whole of your letter is now selected.

● Alternatively, you can move the mouse cursor to the left of your text where it changes from pointing left to pointing to the right. Hold down the [Ctrl] key and click on the left mouse button. The whole of your text is now selected.

4 SELECTING LINES AT A TIME

Selecting blocks of text by lines can save time. Move the mouse pointer to the left of the first line that you want to select. Hold down the left mouse button and move the mouse pointer to the last line of your chosen block. Release the mouse button and the block is selected.

2710 4ᵗʰ Avenue
Omaha
NE 38523

Dear Billy

It was great to hear from you on Thursday. Good to hear you
much worse than the last place anyway! Hope Rebecca's feel

I was speaking to the Jaspers the other day. We really must s
gossip. I can't wait! How about our place? We're free next w
what you think.

Take care

MOVING TEXT – CUT AND PASTE

You can move whole blocks of text either within your document or between documents when using Word. The easiest way to do this is by "cutting" selected blocks of text from your letter and "pasting" them back into a different place.

1 CUTTING TEXT

● Select a block of text ⬚.
● Click on **Edit** on the menu bar. The **Edit** menu drops down.
● Click on **Cut** in the **Edit** menu. Your block of text will disappear, but it is not lost. The rest of the text will move back into place around it.

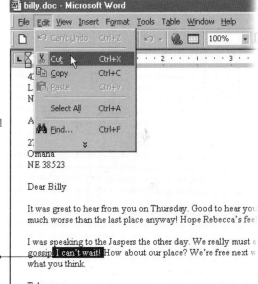

Block of text to be cut ●

Cutting has removed the text ●

24 **Selecting Text**

2 PASTING TEXT

● Position the insertion point where you want the text to reappear.

● Click on **Edit** in the Menu bar, then on **Paste** in the drop down menu.

● The text is pasted back into your letter exactly where you want it.

Dear Billy

It was great to hear from you on Thursday. Good to hear you much worse than the last place anyway! Hope Rebecca's fee

I was speaking to the Jaspers the other day. We really must gossip. How about our place? We're free next weekend. Giv think

Take care

COPYING TEXT

You may want to copy a block of text to a new location while leaving the original block in its old position. Simply go through the cut and paste procedures detailed on these pages, but when you come to cut the text, select **Copy** instead of **Cut** on the Edit menu. The block will stay where it is, but you will be able to paste copies of it whenever you want.

Dear Billy

It was great to hear from you on Thursday. Good to hear you

Dear Billy

It was great to hear from you on Thursday. Good to hear you much worse than the last place anyway! Hope Rebecca's fee

I was speaking to the Jaspers the other day. We really must gossip. How about our place? We're free next weekend. Giv think. I can't wait!

Take care

MOVING TEXT – DRAG AND DROP

This method is a quicker way of moving text around and uses only the mouse. Once you've told Word what part of the text you want to move, you can then "drag" it to the position where you want to move it, and "drop" it into place.

1 SELECTING THE TEXT
● Select a block of text using one of the methods that you have already learned ⌐.

Dear Billy

It was great to hear from you on Thursday. Good to hear you
much worse than the last place anyway! Hope Rebecca's fee

I was speaking to the Jaspers the other day. We really must a
gossip. How about our place? We're free next weekend. Giv
think. I can't wait!

Take care

2 MOVING THE TEXT
● Place the mouse cursor over the block of selected text. Hold down the left mouse button and move, or "drag," the mouse cursor to the position in your letter where you want the text to appear. Don't release the mouse button until the mouse pointer is in exactly the right place.
● Now release the mouse button and the text appears in the new location.

Dear Billy

It was great to hear from you on Thursday. Good to hear you
much worse than the last place anyway! Hope Rebecca's fee

I was speaking to the Jaspers the other day. We really must a
gossip. How about our place? We're free next weekend. Giv
think. I can't wait!

Take care

Dear Billy

It was great to hear from you on Thursday. Good to hear you
much worse than the last place anyway! Hope Rebecca's fee

I was speaking to the Jaspers the other day. We really must a
gossip. We're free next weekend. How about our place? Giv
think. I can't wait!

Take care

24 Selecting Text

CHANGING THE LAYOUT

In this section we deal with how to lay your text out on the page in the way you want it. The most common layout changes that you'll be making are indenting and aligning.

INDENTING THE ADDRESS

1 SELECTING YOUR ADDRESS

● Using either the mouse or the keyboard, select the lines of your address as a block of text ◌.

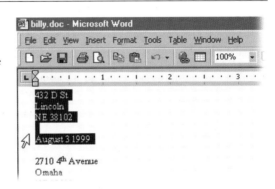

2 CHANGING THE INDENT

● Directly above the text on the screen is a numbered line. This is the ruler.

● Move your mouse pointer to the small symbol called the left indent marker shown at right.

● Click on the box at the base of the left indent marker, and hold down the left mouse button.

Selecting Text

● Drag the left indent marker, by using the box, across the ruler however far you want your address to be indented.

● Now release the mouse button. Your address has moved across the screen.

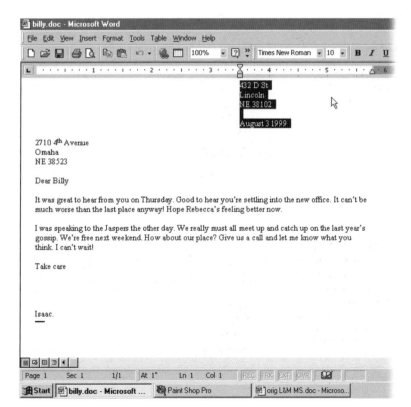

INDENTING PARAGRAPHS

You may want to make each of your paragraphs begin a little further into the page than the main text (a "first line indent"). Or you may want the body of text indented except for the lines beginning each paragraph (a "hanging indent"). These steps take you through how to do each of these procedures.

1 SELECT THE PARAGRAPHS

● Select only the paragraphs of text in your letter and not the addresses, date, greeting, and sign-off.

2710 4ᵗʰ Avenue
Omaha
NE 38523

Dear Billy

It was great to hear from you on Thursday. Good to hear you
much worse than the last place anyway! Hope Rebecca's feel

I was speaking to the Jaspers the other day. We really must a
gossip. We're free next weekend. How about our place? Giv
think. I can't wait!

Take care

2 FIRST LINE INDENT

● Move your mouse pointer over the left indent marker on the ruler 冂.
● When the pointer is on the top part of the left indent marker, hold down the left mouse button.
● Drag the pointer along the ruler to however far in you want the indent.

● Release the mouse button. The first lines of each of your paragraphs are now indented.

2710 4ᵗʰ Avenue
Omaha
NE 38523

Dear Billy

It was great to hear from you on Thursday. Good to hear
can't be much worse than the last place anyway! Hope Rebec

I was speaking to the Jaspers the other day. We really m
year's gossip. We're free next weekend. How about our plac
you think. I can't wait!

Take care

3 HANGING INDENT

● For a hanging indent, go through Step 1 (opposite) to select the text.
● Now, move the mouse pointer until it is over the left indent marker ⌐.
● Position the pointer over the middle part of the left indent marker, (avoiding the other two parts of the left indent marker may need some practice).
● Hold down the left mouse button and drag the pointer over to the right as far as you want the paragraphs to be indented.
● Release the mouse button. Your paragraphs are now formatted with a hanging indent.

2710 4ᵗʰ Avenue
Omaha
NE 38523

2710 4ᵗʰ Avenue
Omaha
NE 38523

Dear Billy

It was great to hear from you on Thursday. Good to hear you
much worse than the last place anyway! Hope Rebecca's

I was speaking to the Jaspers the other day. We really must a
gossip. We're free next weekend. How about our place?
think. I can't wait!

Take care

ALIGNMENT

At the moment all your text except for your address is aligned to the left – the left side is straight while the right is ragged, like text created with a typewriter. Word can make the right side straight as well, like text in a book (this is called "justified text"). Other possibilities include aligning your text to the right, which leaves the left side ragged, or centering the text exactly down the middle of the page.

1 JUSTIFIED TEXT

● Select the text you want to realign.

● Drop down the **Format** menu from the menu bar at the top of the screen.

● Click on **Paragraph** in the Format menu and the **Paragraph** dialog box opens onscreen.

● Click on the drop-down button next to the **Alignment** option. A small menu will drop down.

● Click on the word **Justified** in this menu.

● Click on **OK** and the dialog box closes.

● Your text is now justified with the left- and right-hand sides both straight.

2 RIGHT-ALIGNED TEXT

● Follow Step 1 (opposite) until you get to the **Alignment** drop-down menu in the **Paragraph** dialog box.
● This time click on **Right** and then on **OK**.
● Your text has been aligned to the right.

3 CENTERED TEXT

● Follow Step 1 until you get to the **Alignment** drop-down menu in the **Paragraph** dialog box.
● Click on **Center** this time, then on **OK**.
● Your text has been centered on the page.

QUICK WAYS TO ALIGN TEXT

You are also able to realign text by using the alignment buttons (shown at left) on the toolbar at the top of the screen. First select the text and click on the button you need. From left to right, the buttons mean: left-align, center, right-align, and justify.

APPEARANCE

Your letter now looks better than it did before. However, there are many other tweaks and touches that can transform your text to just the way you want it to appear.

FONT AND FONT SIZE

The font is the kind of lettering that Word uses to display your text. You may wish to use different fonts in different kinds of letter: a stern, professional-looking font for business letters, and a lighter, friendlier font for your personal letters. You may also wish either to increase or decrease the size of the font that you use.

1 THE FONT DIALOG BOX

● Select all the text in the document ⌐.
● Drop down the **Format** menu from the menu bar.
● Choose **Font** in the **Format** menu. The **Font** dialog box opens.

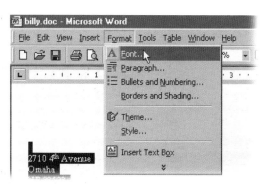

QUICK WAYS TO FORMAT FONTS

You may have noticed that the font, font size, and the buttons for bold, italic, and underline are included in the Formatting toolbar (just above the ruler). To format fonts without using the **Font** dialog box, you can select the text and use these tools to format it. The font and font size are drop-down menus. The font style buttons (shown left) click in or out to show if, say, Bold is on or off in a selected block of text.

2 CHANGING THE FONT

● The **Font** menu is displayed under the **Font** tab in the **Font** dialog box. Scroll up and down it using the scroll bar at the side of the menu. Your text is probably in Times New Roman at the moment.

● As you click on different fonts, the appearance of the selected font is shown in the **Preview** box in the **Font** dialog box.

● Keep scrolling through the fonts until you find one you want to use.

Preview Box ●

3 FONT SIZE

● Now check the **Size** menu at top right of the **Font** dialog box.

● The font size is probably set to 10. This is quite small. Try clicking on **12** or any font size you want – 10 and 12 are the most often used in plain text.

● The **Preview** box will show the new font in its new size.

4 APPLYING YOUR CHANGES

● When you are satisfied with the font and font size, click on the **OK** button.

● The **Font** dialog box will close. Your text is now formatted in the new font and font size.

FONT STYLE

In addition to the regular font, there are three other font styles – bold, italic, and underline – that can be used to emphasize individual words, phrases, or any other block of text. They can also be used in combination for extra effect.

1 BOLD TEXT

● Select the text 🖰 you want to make bold.

● Open the **Font** dialog box from the **Format** menu.

● In the **Font style** menu click on **Bold**.

● Click **OK** to close the **Font** dialog box.

● Your selected text now appears in bold.

Bold text ●——

2 ITALIC TEXT

● Follow Step 1 (opposite), but click on **Italic** in the **Font Style** menu of the **Font** dialog box.

● Click **OK** to close the **Font** dialog box.

● Your selected text is now displayed in italics.

Italicized text ●

Dear Billy

It was **great** to hear from you on Thursday. the new office. It can't be much worse tha Rebecca's feeling better now.

I was speaking to the Jaspers the other day catch up on the last year's gossip. We're fre place? Give us a call and let me know what you

Take care

3 UNDERLINED TEXT

● Select the text and open the **Font** dialog box in the usual way.

● Drop down the **Underline** menu (below the **Font** menu in the dialog box).

● There are many underline options, but the most useful is **Single** – a single line under the selected text. An alternative is **Words only** – each word is underlined, but not the spaces separating them. Click on your choice.

● Click **OK** to close the **Font** dialog box.

● The selection is now emphasized by underlining.

I was speaking to the Jaspers the other day catch up on the last year's gossip. We're fre place? Give <u>us a call</u> and let me know what you

Words only ● *underlined text*

Take care

LINE SPACING

You may want to increase the spacing between the lines of your letter – some find it easier to read. For example, double line spacing creates a space the height of one line between each line of the text. Other options are also available.

1 SELECT THE ENTIRE LETTER

● Click on **Format** on the menu bar to drop down the **Format** menu.

● Click on **Paragraph** from the **Format** menu to open the **Paragraph** dialog box.

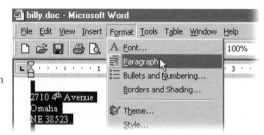

2 LINE SPACING SELECTION

● Click the small down arrow on the right of the **Line spacing** box. The **Line spacing** menu drops down.

● Choose **Double line** spacing from the menu.

● Click on the **OK** button.
Your selected text now
appears with the chosen
line spacing.

3 MULTIPLE LINE SPACING

You are not limited only to
single, 1.5, and double line
spacing when using Word.

● Select part of your text
and click the down arrow
in the **Line spacing** box.
The **Line spacing** menu
drops down.

● Click on **Multiple** at the
foot of the menu.

● In the **At:** box the figure
3 appears. Three-line
spacing is the default
selection for multiple line
spacing. If you want a
different number, highlight
the 3, type the number
of line spaces, and click
on **OK**.

● The lines of your selected
text are now separated by
your chosen line spacing.

STORING YOUR LETTERS

It is usually essential to save your letters on your hard disk so that you can refer to them at a later date. This section provides an overview of how to store and recall your text.

WORKING WITH FILES

A file is what we call any piece of data that is stored on a computer's hard disk. This could be a spreadsheet, a program, or your letter that you have created using Word. Not only can you store (save) your documents when you have completed them, it is important that you also save your files as you work, especially if they are long and you have put a lot of work into them. If your computer suddenly crashes you could lose everything you have done since you last saved your work.

1 CREATING A NEW FILE

● When you open Word, a new file is automatically created in which you can begin typing.
● You may want to create other new files later on. Drop down the **File** menu and click on **New**.
● Click on **Blank Document** to select it and click on **OK**.

2 SAVING A FILE

● Drop down the **File** menu from the menu bar. Click on **Save**.

● If the file has already been saved, the **Save** command will simply save the new version and you may continue typing. If you are saving the file for the first time, the **Save As** dialog box appears and you can assign the document a name and a location.

3 OPENING A FILE

● Drop down the **File** menu from the menu bar. Click on **Open**. The **Open** dialog box appears.

● The **Open** dialog box shows the files you have already saved. Click on the file you want and then click on **Open**.

● The file opens and you may begin working on it.

4 CLOSING A FILE

● You usually close a document when you have finished working on it. Drop down the **File** menu and click on **Close**.

● If you have not saved your text, or if you have changed it since you last saved, you are asked if you want to save the file.

● Click on **Yes** if you have forgotten to save your work. Click on **No** if you're absolutely sure that you don't want to save either the document or the changes you have made since you last saved. If in doubt, click on **Cancel** and return to the document.

5 SAVING THE FILE TO FLOPPY DISK

● Click on **Save As** in the **File** menu to open the **Save As** dialog box.

● Drop down the **Save In** menu in the dialog box.

● Click on **31/2 Floppy (A:)** in the Save In menu.

● Click **OK** and your file is saved to the floppy disk.

WORKING WITH FOLDERS

As you create more files, your hard disk may begin to look cluttered. When you want to open a file, you may not be able to find it because the list of files is so long.

The way to avoid this is to use folders, which can be given names, such as Personal and Finance, so that you know where to store and find your files.

1 CREATE A NEW FOLDER

● When you want to save a document in a new folder, begin by dropping down the **File** menu and click on **Save As**. The **Save As** dialog box appears.

● Click on the button showing a sparkling folder – this is the **Create New Folder** button.

● The **New Folder** dialog box opens. Type in a name for your new folder and click the **OK** button.

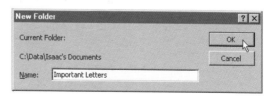

● The **New Folder** dialog box closes. The **Save As** dialog box reappears, this time showing your new, and empty, folder.

2 SAVING INTO YOUR FOLDER

● Type a name for your file in the **File** name text box and click on **Save**. The **Save As** dialog box closes and your file has been saved in the new folder.

3 MOVING WITHIN FOLDERS

● To open the folder containing the current folder, click on the folder icon that contains the right-angled arrow in the **Save As** dialog box – this icon is also in the **Open** dialog box.

So many folders…
You can have as many folders as you want within a single folder, but again, this may become unwieldy. So it might be better to split your folders according to type. You could have a Work folder with a Customer folder and a Supplier folder to divide two different kinds of letters; and a Personal folder with a Friends folder and a Family folder within it. You can of course further subdivide. Utility is the key – create folders only when you think they'll be helpful.

PRINTING

You will want your letter to appear on paper looking as neat as possible. Word has features that let you preview the printout of your letter, make improvements, and finally print your letter.

PRINT PREVIEW

Print Preview lets you see how the printed version of your letter will appear. This is done by showing each page as a scaled-down version of the specified paper size – usually 8½ x 11. The changes you can make in Print Preview include adjusting the margins, but it's not possible to edit the text when previewing. You can preview one page at a time or view several pages at once. Seeing more than one page lets you compare how they look and see how your changes affect your letter.

1 PREVIEW YOUR TEXT

● Open a file that you want to print out.

● Go to the top of the text with the insertion point ⌖.

● Click on **File** in the Menu bar and click on **Print Preview** in the **File** drop-down menu.

● Your screen now shows a print preview of your letter.

┌──┐
│12│ **Insertion**
└──┘ **point**

2 SHOWING MULTIPLE PAGES

● If your letter has more than one page, you may want to see them all on one screen. Look at the Print Preview toolbar (now the only toolbar at the top of the screen). There is a rounded box containing four small rectangles (shown at right). This is the **Multiple Pages** icon.

● Click on the **Multiple Pages** icon, a menu of gray pages appears.

● Move the mouse pointer over the menu to choose

how many pages you want to view. In the example shown, **1 x 2** pages is selected. The first number is the number of rows in which your pages appear, the second number is the number of pages to be shown. The maximum is 3 x 8, which is selected by holding down the left mouse button and moving the mouse pointer right.

● Release the mouse button over the required display.

● You can now see how your letter will appear on the printed page.

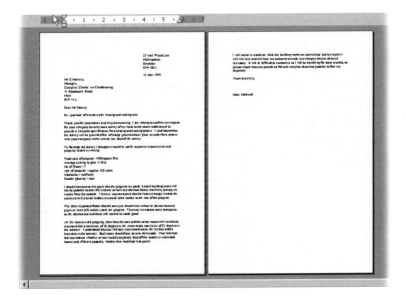

3 PAGE SETUP

● You may want to improve the look of your letter. Perhaps there is not enough room between the text and the edge of the paper. Or maybe a couple of lines spill onto a new page that could fit on the previous page. Both these problems can be solved by changing the margins.

● Begin by dropping down the **File** menu and click on **Page Setup**.

● The **Page Setup** dialog box appears.

4 CHANGING THE MARGINS

● There are boxes in the **Page Setup** dialog box to control the top, bottom, left, and right margins.

● You can increase or decrease the margins by increments of one-tenth of an inch by clicking the up and down arrow buttons to the right of each margin control box. Or click inside a box to enter a size.

● When you have selected the margin sizes, click the **OK** box to see your results.

● When you are satisfied with your changes, click on **Close** in the Print Preview toolbar to return to the normal view of your letter.

PRINTING YOUR LETTER

The actual process of printing out your letter is very simple. The Print Preview feature makes it unnecessary to print a number of draft versions of your letter because you now know how it will appear on the page. All that is left to do now is to use the very simple Print command to produce a hard copy of your letter.

1 THE PRINT DIALOG BOX

● Drop down the **File** menu and click on **Print** to open the **Print** dialog box.

● You can print selected pages of your letter if you want. Enter the numbers of the pages into the **Pages** box under **Page range**.

● You can also print more than one copy of your letter. Enter the number you want into the **Number of copies** box at the right of the **Print** dialog box.

● Check that your printer is connected to your computer and that it is switched on.

● Click on **OK** and your letter begins to be printed.

PRINTING QUICKLY

In most cases, you will not need to "customize" your printing because you simply need one copy of all the pages of your letter. Click on the printer icon in the toolbar at the top of the screen. Your letter is printed without using the **Print** dialog box.

Enter the number of copies required ●—

LET WORD HELP

**Word has many helpful features including a spelling checker, a
grammar checker, a thesaurus, templates on which to base your
documents, and wizards that produce customized documents.**

SPELLING CHECKER

However good your letter looks on paper,
it can be let down by typing errors. Even if
your spelling is impeccable it is inevitable
that some incorrect keystrokes are made.

Word can check your spelling for you as
you type, or you can have Word check the
spelling of your whole document when
you've finished writing it.

1 CHECKING AS YOU TYPE

● Try typing a deliberate
mistake into your letter.
● A wavy red line appears
below the incorrect word.
● Move the mouse pointer
over the word containing
the error and click with the
right mouse button (right
click). A pop up menu
appears near the word.
● Word lists alternative
words that you could have
intended to type instead of
the mistake. Left-click on
the correct word.

Dear Margaret

Thanks for your leter|

Thanks for your leter

letter
later
leer
latter
letters
Ignore All
Add
AutoCorrect ▶
Language ▶
Spelling...

● The mistake is replaced by the correct word and the pop up closes.

Dear Margaret

Thanks for your letter |

2 ADDING WORDS

● Now type something that is correct but obscure and which the spelling checker is unlikely to recognize, such as a foreign word or an unusual name.

Dear Margaret

Thanks for your letter. I've made some calls to but so far no luck. C'est la vie.|

● The word, though not a mistake, is underlined by the wavy red line.

● Right click the word. The menu drops down.

● Click on **Add**. The spelling checker adds the word to its dictionary and will no longer underline the word as a "mistake."

● The wavy red line disappears because the spelling is now accepted as being correct.

Thanks for your letter. I've made some calls to but so far no luck. C'est la vie.

Chest
Crest
Chests
Crests
Cess

Ignore All
Add
AutoCorrect ▶
Language ▶
Spelling...

Dear Margaret

Thanks for your letter. I've made some calls to but so far no luck. C'est la vie.

GRAMMAR CHECKER

Word's automatic grammar checker works very much like the spelling checker. The obvious difference is that Word marks what it believes to be grammatical errors with a wavy green line, not a red line. The grammar checker cannot offer perfect advice due to the complexities of English. So accept its suggestions carefully.

CORRECTING GRAMMAR

● Word has detected a clumsy sentence structure.
● Right-click the sentence and a menu pops up.
● Choose the suggestion or click on **About this Sentence** to have the problem explained. Click on **Ignore** if you think the grammar checker is itself making a mistake.
● If you click on **About this Sentence**, the office assistant, which can be switched on by using the **Help** menu, pops up and explains what Word thinks is the problem.
● Click with the mouse button away from the advice to close the panel.

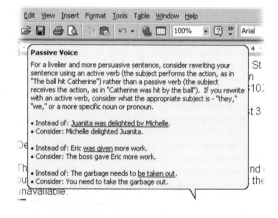

● Right-click the sentence again to display the pop up menu and click on the suggested correction.

r. I've made some calls to try to find out what you st la vie. I was told by Simon that the information

r. I've made some calls to try to find out what you st la vie. Simon told me that the information is

The grammar of the sentence has been revised

THESAURUS

You may want to find an alternative word to express what you mean. The thesaurus feature in Word lists possible words in the same way as the paper-based thesaurus except that it works directly on the word for which you require a synonym.

SYNONYMS

● Place the insertion point in the word for which you want to find a synonym.
● Drop down the **Tools** menu from the menu bar. Click on **Language**.
● A submenu appears, click on **Thesaurus**.

● The **Thesaurus** dialog box appears. Synonyms are listed on the right-hand side.

● Click on a synonym. It appears in the **Replace with Synonym** box.

● Click on the **Replace** button.

● The word is replaced with the synonym.

CHECKING AFTER YOU HAVE FINISHED TYPING

Some people find that having Word checking their spelling and grammar as they type is distracting and intrusive. If you would prefer not to have the wavy red and green underlines appearing below your text, you can turn these functions off.

1 TURNING OFF CHECKING

● To turn off the spelling checker while you type, drop down the **Tools** menu from the toolbar.

● Click on **Options** and the **Options** dialog box opens onscreen.

● There are a number
of tabs at the top of the
Options dialog box for
altering different aspects of
Word. Click on the **Spelling
& Grammar** tab to display
the available options under
Spelling and **Grammar**.

● Click once in the **Check
spelling as you type** tick
box. The tick disappears.

● Click on the **OK** button.
Word will now no longer
check your spelling as you
type. You can still, however,
check the spelling of all the
text in one pass, after you
have finished typing.

● If you wish to stop Word
checking the grammar,
click once in the **Check
grammar as you type** tick
box. The tick disappears
and the grammar checker is
turned off.

2 CHECKING THE DOCUMENT

● Drop down the **Tools** menu from the menu bar.

● Click on **Spelling and Grammar** from the Tools menu. Word will work through your document with the **Spelling and Grammar** dialog box, prompting you at every error that is found.

● If you want to accept a suggested spelling, click on the correct one from the **Suggestions** box and click on the **Change** button.

● If you want to correct the error yourself, click inside the **Not in Dictionary** box and position the insertion point over the error. Make the text correction yourself by using the keyboard and click on the **Change** button.

● If you don't think that there is an error, click on the **Ignore** button.

● Word moves on to the next error in your text until it can find no more and the information box appears telling you that the check is complete. Click on **OK**.

TEMPLATES

Usually when you come to create a new file, either you work from the blank file that Word creates when it is launched, or you create a new blank file by choosing the Blank Document option from the **New** dialog box. This time, you can save yourself some of the work involved in laying out a document by creating a preformatted letter and filling in the blanks. As an example of this, follow the steps below to create a letter using the **Elegant Letter** template.

1 CREATE A NEW FILE

● Drop down the **File** menu and click on **New**.
● In the **New** dialog box click on the **Letters & Faxes** tab and click on the icon labeled **Elegant Letter**.
● Click on OK.

2 FILLING IN THE BLANKS

● Your new file will now be open on the screen.
● Click on the box at the top of the letter marked **Click here and type company name**. The box itself is not printed out - it's only to show you the boundaries of where you can type.

● Click on the line of text that reads **Click here** and **type recipient's address.** You can begin typing the recipient's address – the line of text vanishes when you begin typing.

13 Augu

[Click **here** and type recipient's address]

Dear Sir or Madam:

Type your letter here. For more details on modifying this letter letter, use the Window menu.

Sincerely,

● Using the insertion point or the mouse pointer, select the text of the paragraph that is already in place and begin typing. The old text disappears as you begin to start typing.

13 Augu

[Click **here** and type recipient's address]

Dear Sir or Madam:

Type your letter here. For more details on modifying this letter letter, use the Window menu.

Sincerely,

● Add your name and job title over the lines of text at the end of the letter. Just click in these lines to select them, and start typing.

Sincerely,

[Click **here** and type your name]
[Click **here** and type job title]

● Your address goes at the foot of the Elegant Letter. Scroll down the page and add your address into the address box.

● You have now created a letter using the Elegant Letter template.

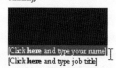

|STREET ADDRESS| · |CITY/STATE| · |ZIP/POSTAL CODE|
PHONE· |PHONE NUMBER| · FAX· |FAX NUMBER|

WIZARDS

Wizards are a simple way of producing formatted letters quickly. There is no need to type names and addresses directly into the letter – Word uses dialog boxes for you to supply the information and then adds this to the letter. You can create the same letter using the Letter Wizard that you did using the template.

1 STARTING THE WIZARD

● Drop down the **File** menu and click on **New** as usual.
● Click the **Letters & Faxes** tab and click on the icon marked **Letter Wizard**.
● Click on the **OK** button.
● A small dialog box appears along with the office assistant.
● Click on **Send one letter**.

2 LETTER FORMAT

● The **Letter Wizard** dialog box opens. There are four steps in the Letter Wizard – the first is **Letter Format**.
● Drop down the **Choose a page design** menu and choose the one you want. You will notice that **Elegant Letter**, the template we used earlier in this section, is one of the designs.
● Drop down the **Choose a letter style** menu and choose from **Full Block** (no indents), **Modified Block** (some indenting), or **Semi-Block** (full, with stylish first line indents).
● Click on the **Next** button to go to the next section.

3 RECIPIENT'S INFORMATION

● The **Letter Wizard** dialog box now shows the **Recipient Info** step.

● Enter the recipient's name and address in the relevant text boxes.

● Choose a salutation from the drop-down menu under **Salutation**, or type in your own.

● Click on the **Next** button.

4 OTHER ELEMENTS

● The **Letter Wizard** dialog box now shows the **Other Elements** step.

● If you want to include a reference line, click on the check box to the left of **Reference line**. A tick will appear in the box. You can now drop down the **Reference line** menu and use the available options.

● Do the same for any other features you want: **Mailing instructions**, **Attention**, **Subject**.

● If you wish to send a courtesy copy, insert the details into the boxes at the foot of the dialog box.

● Click on the **Next** button.

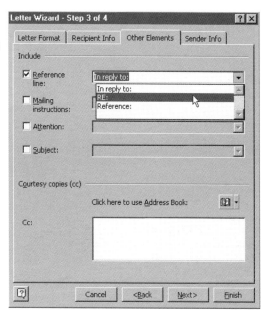

5 SENDER INFORMATION

● The last step of the **Letter Wizard** dialog box is the **Sender Info** step.
● Type your name into the **Sender's name** box.
● Type your address into the **Return address** box.
● Select a closing from the **Complimentary closing** drop-down menu – or type your own into the box.
● Click on **Finish** to allow the Letter Wizard to create your document.

6 START TYPING

● The **Letter Wizard** dialog box vanishes. The office assistant appears and asks you if you want to do any more to your letter.
● Make a selection or click on **Cancel**.
● Your letter is ready. Everything is in place except the paragraphs of main text.
● Start typing as with the Elegant Letter template.

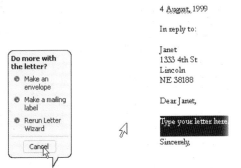

MAIL MERGE

Mail merge is a way of sending personalized letters to a number of people. Although more often used by business, mail merge is useful for telling people about the large events in our lives.

MAIN DOCUMENTS AND DATA SOURCES

So far you have only been working with letters to individual recipients. You may however wish to create a letter to be sent to a number of people – for instance, to notify all your friends that you have moved. You could produce a letter addressed to one person, print it out, change the recipient's name and address, print out the new letter to the next person, and so on. This would however be a very tedious and time-consuming process. To save you this trouble you can use a feature called Mail Merge. This allows you to create a standard letter and a list of names and addresses. The letter and the list are then merged to create personalized letters to everyone in the list. The standard letter is called a Main Document – the list is called a Data Source. Let's start by creating a Main Document from scratch.

1 CREATE A MAIN DOCUMENT

● Drop down the **Tools** menu and click on the **Mail Merge** option.
● The **Mail Merge Helper** dialog box opens.
● Click on the **Create** button under **Main document**.